RENTAL PROPERTY FOR THE BEGINNER –

Managing a project from thought to profit

Michael W. Macon

DEDICATION

This book is dedicated to my dad. I was a pain in his but growing up and then I became just like him. I turned out pretty well considering....

TABLE OF CONTENTS

INTRODUCTION

We have all heard the question, "What would you do if you had no need for anything and would do it for free?" Renovating residential real estate is that thing I would choose. I love the process of taking something that nobody recognizes as having any value and making it a place where I would gladly live.

This book is not about philosophy. I will not suggest you to do this for free. In fact there is good profit and income potential in this type of work if done with purpose and done correctly. You must know that you will not become rich overnight. You will work your tail off. It is work that a lot of others would not try because they do not realize you can make a great return. I am very grateful that I have found something that I love and can also make a great return. In the following pages I will share with you the process and my own experiences.

When I was a young I spent a great deal of time working with my father on our small farm. We kept livestock and raised most of our own food. This type of life makes for many days and hours of work for a young man who, at the time, would have preferred to be out with friends. My father worked a regular job outside the farm and while the farm was not large, it was just big enough to keep us busy in the evenings and just about every weekend doing something, whether it was building something for the place, making repairs, or caring for the livestock. We built fencing, put up barns and sheds, did work in our gardens and fields, and had to be able to fix anything that came up along the way. There was simply not the resources to seek outside help to do these things. I learned at an early age to work on my own car, to feed livestock, raise my food, cut and gather firewood, and do all those things we watch so fondly on reality TV shows today. While I miss much of that life a great deal, at the time I am sure I was not so grateful and pleasant towards my father when having to do all these task. I am sure he remembers more details on this but I do not bring it up for fear of a lecture on that or many other things I could have done better growing up. I will stay in my place of bliss over these experiences.

These experiences taught me to be good with my hands. I had to have the confidence that I could figure my way through just about anything with effort and perseverance. I remember my father telling me once when teaching me to fix something that "if you know how to do this son, you will always eat". It was ingrained in me early to take on things others may not and make lemonade of the lemons in front of me. I apply that same concept and use my interest gained at a young age on construction to renovate residential real estate. I do this because I truly love it. I also do it because it serves as a good way to build a slow and steady business which will creates profit and rental income.

1 – BIRTH OF THE IDEA

I was just out of college when I began to have an interest in real estate investing. I read everything possible on how to enter the business.

This was the era of those late night infomercials showing how to have the life of lavish living in a tropical location of your dreams if you just bought that real estate program. While there were programs and books in which I found value and learned a great deal, the biggest challenge I faced was fear. I read or listened to these programs over and over, frozen from action by the fear of getting caught in something bigger than I could handle. For more than a decade I went on reading and preparing for that day while never fully sure it would every happen.

This book is not a miracle program on how to go about some system which will make you wealthy. There may be systems out there which work but with geography, prices, climate, construction methods, age of available homes, and so many other things so varying, I do not believe there is a single system that will work for everyone. I have always been a logical process driven person. I had to dive in and get myself dirty before I know for sure I can do it successfully. This book is about that process of diving in and how I went, and still go about the process of a property selection and renovation.

If you are as I was, one of your biggest fears is the risk of getting stuck in something that sinks your life ship and you never recover. Biting off something that is way too big for you and being locked into a mess. Well I carried that fear around for years until an interesting and really somewhat unrelated event occurred. This was the turning point for me.

2 – MY TURNING POINT

I went through a phase where I wanted a boat. I still hear people to this day say "the two best days I remember with my boat is the day I got it and the day I sold it". I cannot disagree with them except for what this boat experience did for the rest of my life.

I did not have a ton of extra funds at the time but I had it in my head that I wanted a boat. I found a boat with nice basic hull but needed a lot of work. Turns out it needed a motor which I did not realize at the time, mistake one, but I digress. I purchased this boat and went about the journey to get this boat ready to be on the water. I wanted to take my daughters out tubing and have a blast on the lake. I knew very little about boats. I did have some very good friends who did and they helped me immensely, but the point is I knew very little but I went ahead with this project boat purchase.

This boat needed an absolutely insane amount of work to get it on the water in a condition where I was comfortable miles from shore with my family. In fact my friend and I got stranded more than once making runs testing things. I went through about a year working on this boat. I put a new motor, new steering, and repaired or upgraded numerous things in an effort to get it ready. I finally got it water ready. It was definitely not much but it was able to go out and back pretty well.

Shortly thereafter I had some unrelated things which led me to have to sell this boat. I did not make any money from it but I was able to essentially break even and learned so much about a boat, not the least of which was that I never wanted to own a project boat again. The main point was I had taken the plunge and had survived with only minimal scars. I made an awful purchase, overlooked tons of maintenance items, did hours and hours of work, and was still able to break even. That experience told me it was time to take the plunge I had been putting off for so long into rental properties. I have more knowledge there and even if I made some mistakes along the way, if I buy correctly, and take

a logical approach I was sure I could at least get out even and

learn a ton more. It is time to act, finally…

3 – THE PROCESS BEGINS

The first thing you must do find a realtor. This will be a person with whom you hope to work for the long term. I would recommend you put real effort into seeking the right agent. Reach out to multiple realtors in your local area. Tell them you are looking at potential investment property for rental or resale and get their input. You will have an idea whether you may be leaning towards using cash or seek financing to purchase. The amount of cash you have available and/or the amount of loan you are comfortable with drives a general price range for starting. Tell the realtor this price range. Once you have introduced these points then stop and listen. You will be able to tell pretty fast if that realtor should be scratched from your list.

The right kind of agent for this type of work will tell you about recent deals in your area. They will tell you how the market is going for that price range and type of property. They will likely tell you of other investors with which they have worked. These are all good signs. They will have a search service available where they can notify you of listings meeting your criteria and will offer to add you. All of these indicate a realtor that is one who values an investor. Let's be honest here. We are hoping to find property with a good base but likely older, outdated, and worn, perhaps even mistreated to some degree. These are the properties which allow us the most opportunity for gain in equity and they will probably be listed for a lower price. Realtors work on commission and make more money with higher priced listings. A realtor who knows the value of your relationship will not let a lower price stop them from building a potentially long term relationship. I have worked with my realtor for several years. He has handled many deals both purchase and sale to include my primary home. He has changed companies during our time together yet I have always moved to work with him because he is my agent. That is the kind of agent you want working for you.

If the agent shows the slightest reluctance, then move on to the next until you find one you are ready to call a partner. I cannot overstate how important this is later as you look to repeat the

process after your first success.

4 – WHERE TO START

After settling on an agent you will begin getting emails of listings. When setting the first search settings with your realtor be very broad with your criteria. You will receive notices of new listings, and price or status changes. These notices are the beginning of your education so don't get frustrated when you get tons. You will be able to tighten your criteria over time and will reduce the notices. I would suggest that if you chose a price point you may like then set the criteria to be 125% or more of that price. You learn a great deal from watching the price of homes and how they change over time. Some listings go up at a wish list price and quickly gets dropped to a reasonable price. You will get alerts as the prices change and will see this listings as prices are reduced when one did not sell. You will see ones where the status has changed since it is now under contract. If done right the broad search criteria and the variety of notices will have your email full. You may have the ability to save ones you like. If they are in an area you like, and a style you like, but just outside of your range then save them. They may have a price change later and fall right where you like.

It is important that you be mindful of the areas of your community you like and dislike. You will develop an idea of areas of higher crime, higher taxes, more risk, or too far from you. No matter how beautiful a home, and how low the list price, if it is in the middle of one of these areas you dislike, do not consider it.

5 – THE SEARCH PROCESS

As my search criteria I like to use a minimum of 3 bedrooms and 1.5 baths or more, built a certain year or after, with a list price below a certain amount. This is a pretty broad criteria but works well for me and later we will filter further.

When I get these notices I look them over and save a listing or two as I find ones of interest. When I come to a point where I am ready for the next project I review those saved. Likely some have sold and I find a few that on second thought I should not have saved. After removing those I am left with a few to consider further.

When I chose those I will physically visit I have a more thorough set of criteria I use to select those I pursue. Below I have explained my reason for each. You may find my reason does not apply to your area so you can change it up as it best fits your situation.

- Three bedrooms minimum – A three bedroom is perfect for most of our potential tenants. A couple to a small or medium family can easily live there. This gives you the best market for both renting and resale.

- 1.5 baths or more – with three bedrooms think of that family with children and while they may be able to bathe in a single bath, the parents will appreciate a place to wash up and have their own space to do so. This is for a rental. If you are planning for resale I would suggest this be two full baths minimum.

- Build around a certain year or sooner – this will differ widely based upon your area.

- All or mostly brick veneer – I am ok with the occasional section with vinyl or hardboard siding however I prefer the most of the exterior be brick. This just provides the lowest possible exterior maintenance and is often a sign of a pretty good builder. Your region and building practices may not leave this as an option. In the age range I choose there are enough of these available to keep me busy.

➤ I chose location closely to avoid certain property taxes. Property taxes in my area are often double inside city limits compared to that of a similar home a mile away outside of the city, yet I can rent for the same amount and have less expenses. For resale this may not be as critical.

➤ I don't mind a septic system. It is common on homes outside the city limits. If you are in the city limits I would only choose those with city water and sewer even if for a rental.

➢ I personally avoid pools. I will not even consider a place with an in ground pool. It is a liability and insurance is often more for homes with a pool. Of course this would not apply in an area where it is common to have pools. If a common feature in your area it may even be desired. In my area that is just not the case so a pool is an unusual thing versus a norm.

➢ Foreclosures are fine and I have purchased many, but I avoid short sales. Ask your realtor for advice here but there are too many potential problems leading to delays on short sales so I skip them instinctively.

Remember that every search you review, every home you drive by, every neighborhood or area you learn is a lesson so take your time moving on that first purchase. I do not mean be afraid or over cautious but if you are like me you will be excited to look at homes and have an urgency to find one so you can start. This urgency is the enemy of profit. That urgency is what makes you fall for a place when it simply does not fit the logical model you have chosen. If you do not get an offer on one because you took an extra day to think and evaluate then do not worry. You are in this for the long haul and another will come along. You will be able to find the right one. The right one is exactly what you need for this first one so you see success.

6 – WORKING THE NUMBERS

As far as numbers go, I use a model that seeks to have no more than 60% of the value in a home when I am complete using both the purchase price and cost of repairs. I prefer 50% but will sometimes go as high as 60% if the quality of the deal and value of the end result can be considered closer to the value. If a home is in a location where values are a little better and closer to the real 100% value, you may move up to or slightly over that 60% area.

In addition to this percentage of value I also require it to have at least $100 per month positive cash flow above all possible expenses. I actually pad the expenses I use for this calculation so the real cash flow will be greater than projections. These expenses will include property taxes, homeowner's (landlord) insurance, any debt service, 10% vacancy allowance, 10% miscellaneous, and 10% of the rent set aside to be used towards maintenance. You will likely have little or no maintenance expenses in the beginning because you have just fixed everything but it is a good contingency to build funds for a later problem. As you see if it is not vacant, I do not have miscellaneous expenses, and I have no maintenance then my minimum cash flow grows by leaps and bounds there. I look at a rental to produce at least a little cash each month even if I borrowed the money to buy it. I will not get rich off $100 per month but if I pay all the expenses, make the house payment, get the tax benefit, and have $100 afterwards then I will own the house free and clear at some point and am spending no money each month to have the asset. Keep in mind this $100 is a minimum for me and normally I do better. If I do not have debt service I do much better.

This is an actual example of one of my recent rental locations:

- Value - $95,000
- Max I will put in property - $57,000 (60% of value)
- Estimated repairs - $15,000 (we will discuss how we get this later)
- Max offer price - $42,000

This example was of an actual transaction where the offer accepted was $35,000. I had a little more than I anticipated in repair costs at $18,000 (ended up having to buy a new HVAC unit) and still ended up with $53,000 in the property, well below my max of $57,000

There is another very effective method of calculating your max into a property. That rule says never put more than eight times the annual rent into the property including purchase price and repairs. In my experience this method comes in at or near my percentage model above with the percentage model being a little tighter. I would never, ever go above the eight times rule and you should be good.

The same example as above using the eight times rule guideline:

- Monthly rent - $700
- Annual rent - $8,400
- Eight times annual rent - $67,200

As you will see the eight times annual rent gives you a little more offer room and still leaves you well within bounds. Remember earlier that for a rental property I also look for a minimum cash flow after debt service. If these totals work out great but a property does not give you a minimal amount of cash flow after expenses then you are likely in a poor rent area or have too much debt services or expenses and the deal would still not work. We are looking to have this home be self-sufficient and pay for itself. We are not wanting to take money from our day to day living unless necessary. If it is not covering itself and giving you a minimal positive cash flow it is still not worth it no matter how great the purchase price.

It is important to realize that I calculate how much I put into a property as the <u>amount to purchase materials</u>. I do most of the work myself, nearly 100%. If I have to pay a contractor for work I would include the total with labor in my repair estimate however since I do most of the work myself the repair estimate is mostly materials only. If you are using subcontractors for the majority of the work you will likely have to increase the amount you have into the property. It will likely be necessary for you to go a little above the 60% number to get an offer accepted if contracting out most of the work. I cap there so I have a little more equity which compensates me for my own labor in equity gain. Under no circumstances would I every recommend going above the eight times annual rent for a rental, even if you contracted out the entire project. For a resale you will have to go on comps, and with more guidance from your agent on the potential resale in the area. This is hard work that not everyone can do so make sure you don't fall in love and chase a property too high to make money. While this is a labor of love it is also for rental income and resale profit so have a real exit strategy at the start and you will always be ok.

7 – PREPARING FOR A SITE VISIT

With a broad enough set of criteria, you will get notices of new or changed listings daily. Of those you will find a few in the price and city area you desire. Of those you may find one that will warrant a deeper look. When you see inside of that one, you may be disappointed or may have a potential offer. Be patient and drive by to look at the outside of any you find interesting. You may drive by and not even stop. You may stop and see enough that you just leave. You may walk around twice or three times, look in a window or door, and want to see more. To me it is important not to bother the realtor until after you have looked at the outside at least twice. I will often look at a few in a day and go back a second time to those I find interesting just for an additional look at the outside before I reach my realtor interested in seeing the inside. When you look at a few properties back to back you may find after you have seen a horrible one the next on your list will look amazing by comparison. Only by making a second visit do you see it clearly and realize it is not the diamond in the rough you thought.

This is the method I use to ensure I do not overwhelm my agent with wanting to see so many unnecessary properties. By the time I go to see them I have filtered them down and looked them over multiple times. This also serves me to keep the urgency down because I am not in a hurry. I will often be down to only one or two and can see those quickly to decide if they warrant further consideration or if it should be removed from consideration entirely. Even if I like a place after seeing the inside briefly I will often make yet another visit to the in and outside to determine my repairs list. At this point I have looked at the outside at least two times and have looked at the inside two more times before I am even to the point of making an offer. I tend to take a while to make a final decision but when I do I am committed to the property being a success, I know it will work. Taking so much time is worth it to me so I am sure I am making the right decision. This may seem overkill but it is important because having a clear head and taking multiple looks, especially when you are learning, will save you from missing something.

8 – THE SITE VISIT

I look at certain critical things from the start. If any of these things are not on par with my expectation I move on right away.

- Boarded vacant houses nearby or in the neighborhood

- Look at how well the neighbors keep their home and yard. Look for a sense of ownership.

- Are their signs of children playing or living in the area? Neighbors are the best indicator of how nice the place is to live. If they are comfortable enough to allow their children to play, then you can be comfortable with a future tenant feeling that same way.

- Any evidence of safety or security issues? If you are unsure here it is wise to make a visit during off hours, at night, or on weekends to be sure.

- The roof – it will likely not be new but is it in one piece and functioning? A roof does not kill a deal but is a major expense to include in determining the offer IF you are even willing to deal with it at all

- HVAC – foreclosures are notorious for having the heating and air system either pilfered or altogether stolen. This condition is not a deal breaker but it does affect financing. If you are using a loan then you will not get approved for a conventional loan without a heating source. If you will be using a loan then know this challenge. This is not an issue with a cash purchase.

Look for any major decay. This is itself reasonable to expect, but some levels of this damage indicate something much deeper. An example of this is a soft floor in a bath or kitchen. Is it just water damage or there may be much worse damage to the sub-floor. You must be sure you don't have anything unseen like insect infestations. Termites are brutal little beast and can destroy a place from the inside out. Their damage can be repaired but you had better know they are present put it in your calculations if you are willing to even take on the challenge.

Note: Foreclosures do not have the same disclosure standards in their listings as others because the bank just got the place. They cannot really tell you about the history of the home. Check everything, check twice, and even check a third time to be sure there is not anything beneath the surface like infestations, plumbing issues, rot, etc. that you have not captured in your notes. These are not deal breakers but will absolutely affect your offer so do your homework.

9 – SEEING THE INSIDE

When you go to see the inside you want to have a notebook and pen. Bring a camera and I would not plan to use your cell phone. You should take dozens of photos and do not need to be worried about memory or getting them easily to PC for later use. When I first started I would make very detailed notes of what I encountered and take tons of pictures as well. I later moved to just taking tons of photos and made the list later when not under pressure with my agent there waiting. I also found that I inevitably missed things in my notes but because I had taken so many pictures I could literally recreate the house and my visit with photos. When I say photos I mean that even in a first visit I will stand as far back as I can from both the front and back of the roof taking 3-4 photos across left to right of all surfaces. Later on a PC you can zoom in and look for abnormalities which will give insight on whether to proceed or at least areas you want to look further into before you decide. You will obviously look at all things in detail later even climbing on the roof to look, but if you can avoid wasted time when you see a problem right away and move on then a photo is worth it.

Take photos of all appliances, circuit panel, doors, windows, you literally should capture two to three versions of just about everything. Capture photos of the serial number plates of things like the HVAC and hot water heater. Where the serial number plate is not accessible take a picture of the brand and model of any appliances. This will help you determine the age as there are many resources where you can use a model and serial number to break down capacity, manufacture date, etc. If you know you have to replace these then knowing the specs and capacity from the old unit gives you what you need to estimate a correct price for a replacement (e.g. a 40 gallon gas water heater). If you are estimating your costs and do not remember if it is 30 or 40 and if it is electric or gas you could potentially be off by hundreds of dollars in your repair costs estimate. These simple photos help you go back and take a look to be sure. Take pictures of the breaker panel with the door open so you have a shot of all the

breakers, labelling, etc. Take at least a photo or two of each room

and closet as you will need to be sure you are estimating square

footage correctly and these photos will give you general

perspective to do so. Really just recreate the entire house and

everything you see with both close-up and regular shots of both

the inside and outside you will have it all later to recreate your

visit as you continue the process. You can end up having too few

photos when you have a question later and do not have the item

captures to assist you. You can never have too many photos.

10 – THE WORK BEGINS

Now is where you plan your work and determine your rules for this deal. Go down a list of every room, every wall, entry, everything and make a list of whatever pops in your mind. Look at the photos, add to your list. Look at the photos again, add to your list again. Do not worry about being redundant. Capturing something twice or three times is much better than leaving it out altogether. I find that doing this by room is most effective in this brain storming phase. It is ok to be in BEDROOM1 and say carpet and do the same in BEDROOM2. Do not worry because later you can edit the list to say 'CARPET THROUGHOUT'. At this point it is more important to capture everything, or as close as you can get.

Translate this list into a column or spreadsheet where you can add amounts for each thing to arrive upon a total. For work you can do yourself you will use at least the cost of materials. If you will be contracting work then use a number that corresponds to the cost for the job including materials as you would pay a subcontractor. I might spend $200 on vinyl flooring and another $50 on glue and trim materials. If I have it installed it may be $400 so you would either include the $400 if sub-contracting it out or the material specific cost of $250 if doing it yourself.

Once the list is completed and reviewed multiple times, it is time to put an amount to the work. I find that having it in a spread sheet is the most user friendly way to capture it all for later use. At the bottom of all your repairs add a row called "Miscellaneous". I will explain in a moment but this is very important.

The internet is the best resource here. You can sit in a comfortable chair and with your local home improvement stores web sites displayed and look up a price for each of the items on your repair list. Since you have to pay sales tax on most or all of these items you should round to the nearest number when capturing the amount. An example would be a part that is $59.95 would be included on your list for $75. This way you capture an amount for that extra tax and have a little room in case the price goes up a couple dollars between now and the purchase. Do not obsess about it being accurate to the penny here. This is an estimate. In fact it is better to round up slightly and not worry about looking for the least expensive price at this point. You will shop price later when making the actual purchase. You will find most everything this way but there will still be things like fixing fascia board or a hole in sheetrock that does not clearly translate to an item to search. For these just figure what the board and nails would cost or compound and tape for the sheetrock. I use $25, $50, $100 often in these areas.

I use the materials cost because I look at my labor as being captured in the equity I have in the property. I do this because I like it and not just for compensation for my time but still do not want to do it for free. My equity is my gain for my labor. As you do your estimating the contractor cost, a great resource is your local home improvement store. They have great services where they will install the item for a fee if purchased from them, so while you may not yet be estimating a job you can fairly easily estimate a price per SF for carpet and padding, add a little for tax and add that install fee charged by your local home improvement store to determine how much to include in that "New Carpet throughout" item on your list. If you want to go to the extra length there are also professional resources around estimating jobs. Marshall and Swift makes both a book and an online tool for this purpose. It has been several years since I have used this type of tool but I found it useful until I was able to estimate on my own.

Now for the "Miscellaneous" line item. It should be the last item on your list and should be 10% of the sum total of all the lines above it. It may only be a few hundred dollars and that is ok. It is enough to cover any items you have either forgotten or did not account for in the costs of the repairs. When we calculate the cost of new doors on each bedroom, a beginner will often not include the cost of a new doorknob set and new hinges while having only included the cost of the door. That is an easy mistake but the hinges and hardware sets are nearly as much as the door. If we have this miscellaneous line, we have added enough extra that a simple oversight does not throw off our estimate. I always use this method of calculating costs and have come in under budget most every time wIth few exceptions and even if I came in over budget it is only slight. This method works well for me so long as I stick to my limits I end up profitable. Profit is our primary goal.

11 – WHAT TO EXPECT WHILE SEARCHING

It is easy to get frustrated and let down as you look over and over at homes that are either junk or you look over the numbers and realize they just don't work to make you positive cash flow or profit upon resale. Trust the rules here and do not let that frustration take you over and stop you from finding that first successful deal. You will look at 10 or more just to find one that you might put an offer on. You will likely put in two or three offers before you get one that is accepted. You may even go all the way through to an offer once or twice and have it fall through because something unexpected pops up related to costs, repairs needed, or bank requirements. These are all the signals you are doing it right. Do not get attached to a certain location. Do not get excited and chase the deal with a higher offer than your limit. Do not accept something major discovered that you did not anticipate or include in your repair list unless you are prepared to deal with it. It is not easy to find that house that is going to start you off in business but when you find the right one it will work out well for you and be a great experience. It will start you off on a great journey and makes you a little money as well. If it were easy and low offers on perfect homes were accepted every single day then everyone would be doing it and we would likely not be interested and profit would not be enough for us to consider it. Be patient, be determined, be methodical, and you will be successful.

Realize that every single action you take is a lesson. When you drive to a property and realize the area is not the kind of area you like; you have now determined an area to not make physical visits in the future. When you see a home that is in such poor condition but in the listing it did not seem that way; you realize that some agents take the most flattering photos and those are the only ones put on a listing. I promise you the realtor will never take a photo of the carpet in the back bedroom where the resident kept their dog while at work and put it as the first photo you see on the listing..... Each and every action is a lesson and you learn something new. You will get better and better with each and every action so do not get frustrated at things moving slowly. Slow and careful is ok because we are in this for the long haul and want to get it right.

I have not covered any specific repairs. This book assumes a person has basic repair knowledge or knows someone who does. I have several renovation books which are great. There are numerous DIY type shows, videos, and websites out there to help. If a person has the will, they can find out how to do just about anything nowadays just by searching the internet and reading or watching videos.

I will not offer legal or tax suggestions. I will just say that it would be wise to consider whether you will form a business entity for this or do it under your name. There are differences in the loans available for an individual versus a company, the insurance and tax treatments are different, and there are major differences related to liability. It is not so vital to the process until deed and/or mortgage work is done but it will be at that time. I personally use an LLC for all my work because it has liability protections however that is my choice in my situation and you have to make the right

choice for your situation. Seek the guidance of trusted

professionals in your area.

12 – YOUR FIRST ACCEPTED OFFER

At least the first time you have an offer accepted that you get a licensed home inspector to do a complete inspection for you. If you are able to negotiate the seller to pay for that inspection then great. If not I would do it for the first one anyway even if at your own cost.

Be there when they do the actual inspection. They are usually great people who love to share their experiences. They will likely walk you through everything as they are doing it. This will be one of your best education experiences because you will see things through another set of critical eyes and may catch something that you missed. After the first property you may feel comfortable enough to go on your own but that first time consider it an insurance policy and a lesson on how inspections are done. The inspector also provides you a detailed report on their findings with photos and feedback. It is not a bad idea to do these on every offer but at least the first one or two without exception.

Once you have received the inspection report you will have one of three reactions; 1) yeah that is what I saw, 2) I did not catch that and I cannot proceed, or 3) I did not see that but it does not nix the deal. I will have to ask for a price adjustment.

The first two of three above are self-explanatory. I will give you an example of how number three happened to me. I had a foreclosure where all the copper pipe had been cut out and taken to the scrapyard. This was a nice home (I still have it and is rented) and everything else was as I had anticipated but no plumbing. It was cut off at every stub, at every sink, at the water heater (the hot water heater was gone as well), and where it entered the house – nothing! Every bit of copper pipe under this house had been long removed. This sounds like a huge discovery on the face of it and a potential deal breaker. I had not included anything of this repair in my estimates because I did not catch it. I just happen to have the tools and ability to re-plumb the entire house for under $300 in materials. (This is not a huge house so that figure may not hold true for you. This is just an example). I went to the seller and asked for a $1,500 price reduction to cover the cost of that plumbing and the hot water heater that was missing... they accepted! I bought a $400 water heater, $300 of plumbing supplies for a total of $700 and saved $1,500 on the purchase price. Now that I think about it I probably should have asked for $2,500 off!!! In this case the plumbing system is a very vital system and now that it had been discovered missing, the selling agent would have had to put it on the listing going forward. That would not bode well for future offers so while they had me on the hook they worked with me and we came to a reasonable solution that worked for both our needs. Not all situations work out so positive but it goes to show that the possibility does exist.

13 – CLOSING DAY

If you do not have photos of everything as we discussed earlier, well shame on you for not following the suggested outline, but get them now without question. You will use these photos throughout to remember details to better plan materials purchase, etc.

Be ready day one with a new set of locks. Be mindful these locks are the ones that will secure the place during your renovation. They will likely not be the final ones you place upon sale or rent because they often get paint and such during the repair process. I would get secure ones but not kill the bank. This is a good set to remove and plan to use later for the next property for just this same purpose.

The first few days will be when you do the absolutely vital triage. Clean overflowing gutters causing water damage, cover broken windows, disconnect any questionable electrical connections so they are not fire hazards, look for any safety or security issues, and basically do everything vital to stop further

damage until you get to the final fix. This will freeze that damage

in time until you can get back to it in your normal renovation

process. Since you made a list earlier, you will have an easy

reference to identify these triage items soon after closing.

14 – BUILDING IMPORTANT RELATIONSHIPS

Now that you will be coming and going from this property, it is important that you introduce yourself to the neighborhood. Go to the neighbors on either side, behind, or across the street and introduce yourself. Make it brief and do not disclose anything major as to your plans except that you do this part time and would appreciate them keeping an eye on the place for you. Tell them what your vehicles look like and welcome them to reach you if they see anyone else around. Give them a contact number in case anything comes up. This will be your best defense against anything unexpected. The neighbors are there and watch out for one another and will do the same for you. Keep these relationships nurtured during the entire process because these neighbors will be some of your best advocates.

15 – DIGGING IN

You have gotten any serious issues stabilized and have met the neighbors. Now you have a major project to begin. Fortunately you made a list of the expected repairs when you were determining your repair costs and max offer. On this repair list you placed the item and a price beside it. Now I want you to take it and add to it two columns; a priority and a rank. At the bottom of the list add some blank lines and type in the heading "materials needed". As you are planning your next tasks it will be easy to add a shopping list of what is needed next right on the bottom of this list and you will have everything all in one document.

Here is an example punch list:

ITEM	Cost	PRIORITY	RANK
Remove carpet	$0	A	1
Remove bath sink	$0	A	2
New bath faucet	$40	B	2
Replace sliding door	$400	B	3
New kitchen Vinyl	$300	C	4
Paint	$400	C	5
Items needed:			
Bath faucet			
Sliding door			
Kitchen Vinyl			

Your actual list will be much longer but this gives you a suggestion of a format which could be used and the purpose the list should serve. You will simply delete an item from the list when complete, change the priority of an item as it becomes more critical, and add additional items needed as they pop up. I personally do these updates each day and reprint this for my next day just as I would a day planner. I keep the cost column for much of the project to know how much more I will look at putting out to get the place ready. Later in the process when I have made most all the material purchases I often delete the price column because this will then become more of a to-do list. This way you are always current with what you have to do and what is the very next thing. This single sheet will be the most valuable tool of all to manage the project. Do not count on remembering. If you are at the job and something crosses your mind simply capture it in the margins or on the back of the page so you remember to add it to the official list later when you update.

16 – DEMOLITION

Once you have the triage done It is time to gut everything. Choose how to handle the debris removal. There are companies who rent dumpsters and take it away when you are done. A lot of people use them but I priced those early on and found it was much more expensive than my tastes. I have a trailer I leave on sight and load debris on as it is removed from the house. When I am ready I just hook to the trailer and head to the landfill. If I don't get the load to the landfill it just sits until I can get it there.

Until you know what you are dealing with in terms of any harmful materials, it is wise to wear some kind of breathing filter when you remove carpet, padding, flooring, and such. You may also want to wear gloves because you will find sharp corners, nails, and who knows what in the strangest places. You do not want to be breathing the fumes, dust, or debris from this process because it will be very dusty and even if not of harmful nature it is still not healthy in general. Once I have removed all the floor coverings I personally use a yard sprayer filled with 50/50 bleach to water and spray all the floors as a precaution to kill anything which may be present. A light soaking of bleach water on a strong sub-floor will help and should not ever hurt. Bleach is the cheapest and most effective disinfectant I have ever found. It kills germs, mold and mildew, just about any of those things you do not see but may be there.

When gutting a space it is very important to be mindful of what you will be able to keep and reuse or what might be a candidate for donation. If you plan to put new vinyl in a bath you may still be able to use that toilet and reinstall it after the new flooring. If not then you may be able to donate it to your local habitat location. They perform a great service for many and would appreciate the donation, not to mention you get a tax deduction for it as well. So only throw in the demolition pile what you plan to discard. Anything you may reuse or could donate just stage it to one of the bedrooms for later.

17 – APPROACHING THE PROJECT

There are primarily two approaches to this type of project. One is to move room by room with your renovation. This is a method used by many but I am not very fond of this approach and prefer the second which is to do the same part of the process throughout the entire house before moving to the next part of the process. By choosing this second approach you do not finish a room and instead finish an aspect of the renovation at a time. If you are patching sheetrock then you patch all the sheetrock in every room, painting – paint every room and so on. With the second approach you will need more vision to keep you motivated because you may not be able to recognize that the process is moving along because it seems slower this way. I just prefer to do a part of the project and be done with that part before moving on. The idea of sheetrock work or paint in a single room to get that room presentable and then going to the next room starting over is frustrating to me. Some people like seeing the success of that first room move quickly and find it motivates them. It also keeps you from rework, and from possibly ruining what you have already done. There is nothing worse than doing the floor in a room and having to paint later. If you know you have to do floor and paint then do the paint first in the entire place, and then you have no worry about getting paint on the floor because you are replacing it anyway. When I am installing new faucets I do all the bath sinks, the tubs, showers and the kitchen all at the same or around the same time. That way I can get the right plumbing parts in one trip for all. If I forgot something then I get all that is left in one single follow-up trip instead of doing the same for each sink as I work on that single room. Then when you get to floor you can be putting in vinyl at the same time you are ordering the carpet installed, etc. You can tell which way I prefer but you have to have your own approach and either way is just fine and will get the job completed.

18 – WHAT IS A HOUSE REALLY?

A house is essentially a box where electricity enters to the panel and is then distributed to each room, water enters going through the entire house, to the water heater, and back to each sink where there is a non-pressure side to let the water fall back out to septic or sewer system. This is an over simplistic view but once you have down the idea of how the plumbing and electrical come in and the way they connect to all the switches and faucets, the rest is just wood, nails, coverings, and fixtures.

You would start with the plumbing and electrical. These are things you will need during the rest of your work so get them done early and correctly so you have them to use and will also have plenty of time to ensure they are properly working. These larger tasks at the beginning of the process are beneath the surface and invisible to the onlooker. You will not see much physical change when working on these systems but you will have a very vital part done and will be ready when you get rolling to the finish phase and start paint, flooring, and bath finish.

To me the electrical and plumbing are such vital mechanical systems that after you get those complete you are thereafter pretty much in finish mode save for a structure or subfloor repair. If you had to open a wall to get at plumbing or electrical, then you are now closing it after the repair. Once you close the walls, you are looking at the paint, ready to put on a wall finish.

19 – PUTTING IT ALL BACK - BEGINNING THE REHAB

Because we are starting a new business, we want to be prudent and cautions in every part we do. It is wise to only make purchases at or near the time you plan to use them. There are a couple situations which may be exceptions and we will discuss them later. If you are working this as a part time thing, which I highly recommend to start, then you will likely have certain days of your week which you plan for this work. I would not recommend buying so tight that you are in the store every day because you will leave little time for the work but remember we are trying to tie up as little money along the way as possible so we make this successful financially and do not affect our style of living otherwise.

I would recommend you plan your purchases in a couple ways. Firstly go ahead and get the tools or supplies you know you will need regularly at the start. If it is a basic tool and you will need it then be sure you have it. I am not referring to the extravagant things but general power tools and basic hand tools which you know you will soon need. Go ahead and get the supplies you know you will need soon. This will not be a huge list but will be vital things so that when you go to reach for a simple tool, you have it. That will save you time on the job.

When you have that circular saw, that miter saw, hammer, a level, pliers, nails, screws, and all the basics you will able to conquer the world! Well, maybe not conquer the world but you get the point, if you will need a basic tool then go ahead and have it from day one. Do not go overboard if you are beginning. Basic hand tools, a reasonable miter saw, a good drill and bits, and a very good circular saw will take you a very long way. I have actually fully renovated a 1500sf home and the only power tools I had being a circular saw, and a drill. All the rest were hand tools. You can even get away without a miter saw if you want to use the circular saw in that role. I have done it. When you are starting out it is amazing how much you can accomplish with minimal tools. Again, if you have more or have the means to get those extra items then by all means do but if you not able to yet that does not mean you cannot make this work.

I would always buy all you can think of for the next major step or two each time you shop. It is most often the best to get the more basic tool and the smaller package size of supplies. For example, 5lbs of nails may be a little less per pound but if you are only going to need a dozen nails then a pound will be less money paid out, will be easier to transport, and will leave you with less left after to store. This approach will save you a lot as the project goes on and you have less left over when the job is done. Don't get caught up in the idea that you will use it later because that may be true but the most important thing is to not tie up unnecessary resources today.

Since you are now keeping a punch list with priorities it is easy to capture the items needed from this list and make a trip to the store at the end of your regular work day or the beginning of your trip to the renovation site. Always purchase for what you know you will definitely be doing the next day or two and begin getting the following items as they become a higher priority. This will keep your cash for supplies going out steady but not in huge chunks, and will not tie up funds unnecessary until the supplies will be needed. This financial approach will help you in many ways, not just in funds but also it will keep you having minimal returns as you have changing ideas during the process. If you change a color or material type in your plan and have not purchased it yet then no problem. If you have a cut piece of vinyl or 20 gallons of mixed, paint and change your mind then... hundreds of dollars down the drain. It is also important to mention here that you will vary your approach and change your mind along the way, especially the first one you do. It is natural and is part of the learning process.

20 – HOW I CHOOSE AND PURCHASE MY MATERIALS

You will find your home supply store has a large selection of colors, textures, styles, and costs of materials. For most of our purposes in rental property you will go with the economy or perhaps one step above bottom for most materials. This will be different if you are working on a high end property or for resale but for rentals the low to middle of the price spectrum works great for material. You will find great warranties and they will produce great results. When I say low end it is important to keep the end in mind when selecting materials. You would not select vinyl flooring that lasts half the life just to save 10 cents a foot. If you move up that 10 cents you may have 5 more years of life and may have a much easier time with installation and maintaining it. In this example the 10 cents per SF would save you in the long run when you get 10 years of life from the product versus 5 years for the lesser.

One exception to my purchasing as I go approach relates to offers occasionally available from your local home supply store. If you have a store credit card from one of these stores you will sometimes get for 0% interest for 6-12-18-even 24 months with certain levels of qualifying purchases. Some of these places also have discount coupons for a % off your purchase. Many have discounts for current or retired military as well as other groups. I have many times made a list of every item I could possibly think of needing over my entire project list and get them all at once to receive the percent off and the zero percent offer. The purchase as you go approach is meant to not overextend you or cost you in terms of interest and if you have an offer like this available the bulk purchase does neither so it offers a great way to purchase. So long as you have a place to store that lumber, sheetrock, paint, doors, hardware, etc. that is a great way to save. You get the supplies you need, get a discount, and possibly get zero interest for a period of time. This is also a great option for those without tons of cash. It allows you to put off the outlay of cash for a period with no interest and perhaps with a percentage discount

as well. This is also a great way to come in under your repair

budget as you estimated at full price and have saved a

percentage instead. We are starting out here and every single

dollar saved matters and helps us make this a success.

21 – SITE SECURITY

While I have many times bought a few thousand dollars of materials in a single purchase using the discount methods mentioned in the last chapter, it is very important that you be mindful of security. You are working on a location that you are not at all the time. No matter what you do and how great the area is, there are times when petty opportunists will try and take your stuff. Under no circumstances should you store these items purchased ahead or any tools at the home. I am telling you from personal experience. I had made large store purchases and stored purchases and tools at my home sites for many years with no trouble at all. Then that all came to an end. After my working for months on a house with items always left on site, I had a break in one overnight. They took most of the materials they could carry and all my hand tools as well as the couple of power tools I had there. It took a large chunk of funds to replace the tools and supplies, and a long time to get over the feeling of being violated.

From that point I did not leave anything on site and never had any more trouble. So let this be one of those times where I have made the mistake and learned so you don't have to. Just get some containers and some 5 gallon buckets and keep your tools in those and you will be just fine. Bring materials as purchased or from your storage as the project requires.

22 – NEARING INSIDE COMPLETION

You are progressing well and on your way to making this house a home. Neighbors will ask how the work is going, what you plan to do with the place, and when you will be finished. You might also find general discussions about your floor plan and finish coverings choices versus what they have in their home. They will tell you exactly what a future potential buyer or renter would expect in the home. Listen closely and they will give you valuable hints.

As you are nearing the final floor coverings, trim and fixture installation it will be necessary to begin serious planning of your outside punch list items. Major outside repairs will often have been completed early on in the triage to stop allowing in the elements. The outside list will include many "to do" items and not just repairs. It is not uncommon to have your list include raking leaves, filling in a hole in the yard, etc. If you have done the job correctly and timed the work right you will likely have mostly cleaning and presentation type activities like paint, pressure

washing, and landscape remaining. As you begin to plan this

outside work your mind will likely come up with a hundred other

little inside things. Just be patient and capture every single thing

you think of so it gets completed. This is where you think of a

million things you should have done. When you get them on your

list you may later realize they take very short times to complete or

you really do not need to do it at all after thinking it over. You will

be on the outside in no time.

23 – DONE WITH THE INSIDE, NOW WHAT?

As you finish the final touches inside it will be very important to know your final plans with the place. If you plan a sale then you should get your punch list together and visit with your realtor right away. If you knew the home would be sold from the start when you chose your materials and such then you are good to go. If you went part of the way preparing to rent and changed your mind, or was not sure until later in the process then the details will be different if you plan to sale versus rent.

If you are selling the visual aspects are incredibly important as it relates to the landscape, paint and presentation. You simply cannot skimp if you want to maximize your sale price. If you plan to rent the paint and such will not be as vital so long as it is presentable. For a rental you will want to have things like a working mailbox, new locks, landscape cut off at the ground or trimmed back for a resident. Even a little thing like shower curtain rods are normally brought to a home purchased but if I am renting

I prefer to put them myself so I can be sure they are properly anchored in a stud versus my tenant making a hole in the wall pulling a towel off a rod having not install the rod properly. For my rentals I put a screen for bath sinks and not a plunger where the sink cannot clog. This may seem small until you think of a child who leaves the water on in one of your rental homes and the carpet is destroyed by a sink overflowing water into the entire house. If it cannot be clogged it cannot over flow. This is small but important. Another little thing I do in rentals is put adhesive door pucks on every wall where a door knob will likely be opened firmly against my newly painted walls. I put door stops on the hinges as well but they can give. This will keep knob shaped holes from being knocked in your walls. You always want a home to be presentable at the end regardless of your intent but the little details I like to use for a rental differ slightly. It requires a few more parts and a little more work but keeps me from having to redo a lot of the items again later through repairs when a tenant moves. If you are renting then think function and how it will be used. Do the little things to keep the home from being destroyed

by a tenant inadvertently.

24 – GET READY TO RENT

If you plan to rent this is when you get a FOR RENT sign in the yard. A large sign the size of a realtor sign is best and available at your local home store. Put your number and it is helpful to put the beds and baths in a spot as well. Your phone number in the blank with beds and baths included by something simple like "3/2" works perfectly. This little extra will keep people looking for a different beds and baths from wasting your time with a call. For some reason that little set of numbers is fully understood by most who see the sign so you really need nothing more.

When you put this sign out be prepared to get calls, be prepared for the neighbors to ask you questions, and be prepared for people to stop while you are working outside and ask to see the place. Put the sign as soon as you have the inside in a state where are comfortable walking someone through for a look. Minor things which would not be noticed in a walk through are fine but have the inside in the general state where the tenant would

receive it other than perhaps a general cleaning. This is where

neighbors will become such an asset. They will have friends or

family who they have told about your place and how close you are

to renting. They will be one of your best sources to get potential

tenants. Do not procrastinate getting that sign out as soon as you

would be comfortable walking a potential tenant through the

place. It does not have to be ready for a tenant to move in. It only

has to be good enough for a quick walk through for those

interested. Do not delay, get that sign out. Did I tell you to get the

sign out?

It is fine if you are still working outside because the potential

tenant will see the quality of your work inside and assume the

outside will be done as well. The outside is also not as important

to a tenant so long as the place is kept, safe, and maintained.

Each time I have gotten my sign out as soon as I moved to the

outside I have had an easy time finding a tenant. You may be

surprised because they may want to move in even quicker than you were thinking so do not be surprised how well this works for you. I have never had to advertise a place for rent more than the sign I just described. In most cases I put the sign out early in the month as I move to outside work and have a new tenant moving in by the first of the next month.

As you are done with the inside it is also important that you capture a new set of photos. Go crazy and get multiple angles of everything as you did in the beginning but be sure you capture everything. It is critical that you do this now. As you get to outside and people start approaching you to rent it is incredibly easy to forget them altogether. The reason these photos are so important is a few fold but primarily three major reasons. First you will want a record of your work and may like to develop a before and after portfolio. It will be fun to review this portfolio with your friends and family to see the transformation. It also may be useful later if you seek funding or for a business plan. Second, and most important, you want to document the improvements for insurance purposes so you have clear evidence of the improvements in case of a claim. These photos will also serve as documentation of the condition prior to a tenant move in. This will become important later if there is damage and you need proof it was not that way when they moved into the place. You should also take photos just the same way between tenants as one moves out and just before the next moves in for exactly this same reason.

You must have what monthly rent you will expect and what security deposit you are requesting. If done correctly you will have likely determined the rent you are looking for when you analyzed the cash flow in developing your offer. Many people use a month's rent as an additional security deposit. If you use rent as a guideline for your security deposit it is important to be clear. Your tenant must understand that security deposit is not the last month's rent. This is meant to secure you. We will go into that later. Be ready state the rent and deposit to the neighbors and when you receive inquiries.

25 – POTENTIAL TENANTS – DO YOUR HOMEWORK

I am about to cover some of my experiences related to tenants. I again say it is very important to check with your own trusted and qualified professionals to ensure you are following all state and federal laws, codes, and municipal guidelines.

Applications and leases are contracts and are required to meet criteria based upon your locality. Your realtor may be of assistance here if there are specific forms available to meet your area guidelines. Have every potential tenant complete an application. Be sure you ask the right questions. It is best to get at least two years of history from applicant and co-applicant. Ask them for landlord and employment history for at least the last two years and include a statement for them to sign on the application authorizing you to do a credit check and verify the landlord and employment information. Do not think your tenants just seem so nice there is no need to question what they have said. Do yourself a favor and verify their application information. Call their current and/or prior landlord and ask if they were good tenants and did they keep the rent paid. Did they take good care of the place they rented? You may find an occasion where a prior landlord is reluctant to answer. Most will be honest with you. If they do not want to tell you then, it my experience, they may have something less than positive to say and are not saying. People are more than happy to give a positive reference. If they are not willing to say anything at all then that lack of response may say a great deal. You arrive upon your own conclusions. Also call their current employer. There are often rules or policies around what an employer can and cannot tell you. All you are really looking for is that they are truly working there so you know they have the ability to pay rent.

A note on credit checks. I get tenant permission to perform a credit check on each of my applications. The reality of today's economic climate is that many do not have perfect credit and you have to ask yourself do you really care about their credit score. So long as they have been a good tenant at their previous rentals, have a job, are able to pay you rent, and will be a good tenant for you then does a score matter? If they have all that going for them who am I to judge a score on a credit file. While my practice may change in the future, unless there is something unusual I normally do not do credit verification so long as I can get satisfactory reference from their past landlord and current employer.

There are many resources both for free and for a fee with potential lease forms available. Your realtor may have access to your specific realtor association form. As I mentioned on the application, see your own qualified professional for assistance on this and other forms to ensure you have covered yourself and have met local requirements.

26 – STICK TO YOUR PLAN

This is a tentative moment for you. You have worked hard on a renovation. You deserve pay for your hard work but are also nervous because a renter who is interested seems like a sure thing and you need a tenant. You just finished and nobody but you has really looked at the place. You think it is a wonderful job but what will others think? If I get someone interested should I low ball rent? I really need to get a renter in this thing quick. Should I "work with them" on the deposit so I get someone in it right away? What if I don't find anyone who will rent it? I have worked so hard and done such a great job but now all these uncertainties…

Ask a market rent for your place. If you chose to be on the lower end of a reasonable rent spectrum that will be ok but do not drop below a reasonable level. This time of uncertainty is normal. Stick to your plan! Do not feel you have this house and someone needs a place and cannot quite afford it but you will help them out. A moment of kind heartedness will cause you much grief later. Keep in mind all the hours of sweat and tears. How many times did you hit your thumb with the hammer? You deserve to get the market rate of return for your work. Hold out and stick to your plan.

27 – SECURITY DEPOSITS

Do not be reluctant to ask a new tenant for a proper security deposit. Even a great tenant will have an unexpected dent in a wall, a screen torn out, or a cracked window. In addition to fully cleaning the place and returning it to reasonable condition the deposit is intended to cover these things. I have had tenants live in one of my rentals for years. I felt like we were friendly and got along well. I would have helped them in any way possible but when the time came for them to move it was as if all that history went away in a flash. At the moment a tenant plans to move out it does not matter how friendly you were. It is about business and if they have nothing at risk by leaving damage then you will be left holding the bag. Do not put yourself in that place, ever. There is nothing worse than having a terrible tenant who damages a place more than their deposit leaving you to figure out a way to get them to pay you when they are already moving out or gone completely. This is a losing proposition so do not put yourself in that position.

Tenants have pets. We all like pets. You must include in your lease limits as to what types of animals and how many your tenant may keep. I personally include outside only in my lease and the tenant must make a non-refundable pet deposit. Even an outside pet will end up causing some damage or require extra cleaning upon move out. Do not hesitate to get what is necessary to secure possible future repairs. If they are outstanding tenants and you do not have damage then you will be able to refund them any unused portions of deposits. Be wise at the start instead of stuck with expensive repairs on your own dime later.

Very early on in my experience I did not worry about pet deposits. I did not worry about including how many pets or what type of pets a tenant could keep. It was not a huge deal. I was grateful to have a tenant. I had just gotten outside of one of my houses and had not even put up my 'For Rent' sign when an interested person stopped and asked about the place. This was only the second property I had ever done. It was all relatively new

to me. I firmly told her the rent and she was interested. Wow! I did

not even have to drop it at all. I told her the deposit, she agreed.

Nice! She wanted to move in right away. I was done with the

inside and was still finishing the outside as she moved in. Of

course I had a lease but had not bothered to include that

unimportant pet stuff. This is a single family home in a subdivision

on a small lot with a fenced yard. I was proud of my work and she

lived there for a while, overall a good tenant. She had a little dog

but she kept the place clean and paid her rent on time so no

worries. One month I stopped by to get rent and missed her. She

was not home. I had pulled in the drive to turn around and I was

backing out. I looked in the backyard. I thought to myself, "Did she

get a new dog? That is a very weird looking dog in the back yard."

I had backed out of the drive and was pulling away and I had to

go back and look. "I must see that dog", I thought to myself. I went

back to the fence at the side of this house to look. I could not

believe my eyes. She had a horse. A freaking Horse!!!! I stood there for a minute in amazement. I took some photos on my phone, of course I sent the picture right away to a couple friends for a laugh. My tenant had a horse in a fenced in yard in a subdivision. When I finally met her for the rent I asked her about it and she said yes and gave me some song and dance about trying to find another place for it. After I reviewed her lease I realized there was nothing I could really do. There was not an association with rules against this. I had not put anything regarding limits or requirements on pets in her lease.

Ok so I have not told many about that little (but completely true) story to make the point. Put pets in your lease. Put what you expect and you will not allow. Get a pet security deposit from them. Don't end up with a horse!!!!

28 – ALL DONE, WHAT NEXT?

At this point you have a great new tenant. You have an air tight lease and addendums meeting all local requirements. You have modernized a home which is ready for your new tenants to move into. If you have done this correctly and repaired the right things you will likely have years with little maintenance required. Approaching properties this way I have had 5 years or more pass with minimal maintenance and only touch up and paint between tenants.

It is now time to take a deep breath and recognize your success. You have worked hard. You have turned what was an old run down place into a modern home. You are helping a family with a place to live. You have learned tons and have created a location that will make you profit. Be proud of your work. Realize that this is your first and you will get better each time. You have finally taken the plunge and have made it a success. Great Job!

If you enjoyed it as much as I do after a small break you will get the itch and will want to start the search over for the next project. Be patient. Take your time. Apply the additional lessons learned on this first property.